Our purpose at Howard Publishing is to:

- *Increase faith* in the hearts of growing
  Christians
- *Inspire holiness* in the lives of believers
- *Instill hope* in the hearts of struggling people
  everywhere

Because He's coming again!

Published by Howard Publishing Co., Inc., 3117 North 7th Street, West Monroe, Louisiana 71291-2227

99 00 01 02 03 04 05 06 07 08   10 9 8 7 6 5 4 3 2 1

Library of Congress Cataloging-in-Publication Data
Circle of Friends : a treasure of inspirational thoughts for your
    circle of friends / Point of Grace (Denise, Heather, Terry, Shelley).
        p. cm.
    ISBN 1-58229-057-1
    1. Christian women—Religious life. 2. Female friendship—
Religious aspects—Christianity. I. Jones, Denise. 1969–   .
II. Point of Grace (Musical group)
BV4527.C532 1999
248.8'43—dc21
                                                                    99-22751
                                                                       CIP

Circle of Friends. Words and music by Douglas Kaine McKelvey and Steve Siler, ©1996 River Oaks Music Co. (BMI), admin. by EMI Christian Music Publishing (50%) /Magnolia Hill Music (ASCAP) (50%). Used by permission.

Edited and compiled by Philis Boultinghouse
Cover and interior design by LinDee Loveland
Photography on page 15 by Hope Crockett
Photography on pages 20, 21, and 28 by Chrys Howard
Photography on page 48 by Judy Howell

To

_____

From

_____

Date

_____

In a circle of friends we share this prayer: That every orphaned soul will know and all will enter in to the shelter of this circle of friends . . . In a circle of friends we have one Father. In a circle of friends we have one Father.

Circle of Friends

A
Treasure of
Inspirational
Thoughts for Your
Circle of Friends

POINT OF GRACE

and their circle of friends

denise • heather   terry • shelley

HOWARD
PUBLISHING CO.

Circle of Friends

Performed by Point of Grace
Song lyrics by Douglas McKelvey
Music by Steve Siler

We were made to love and be loved
But the price this world demands will
cost you far too much
I spent so many lonely years just trying
to fit in
Now I've found a place in this circle of
friends

In a circle of friends we have one Father
In a circle of friends we share this
prayer
That every orphaned soul will know
and all will enter in
To the shelter of this circle of friends

If you weep, I will weep with you
If you sing for joy, the rest of us will lift
our voices too
But no matter what you feel inside
there's no need to pretend
That's the way it is in this circle of
friends

In a circle of friends we have one Father
In a circle of friends we share this
prayer
That we'll gather together no matter
how the highway bends
I will not lose this circle of friends

Among the nations, tribes, and
tongues we have sisters and
brothers
And when we meet in heaven, we will
recognize each other
With joy so deep and love so sweet
Oh, we'll celebrate these friends and a
life that never ends

In a circle of friends we have one Father
In a circle of friends we share this
prayer
That it will not be long before all will
enter in
To the shelter of this circle of friends

The story behind the song

In a sense, songwriting is like running an adoption agency. Some songs, you feel confident, could be matched with almost anyone, and so you send them out the door at once. Other songs need time to mature and grow. But a song like "Circle of Friends" you just have a feeling about from the very start, and you simply hold on to it until the rightful parents come along to claim it. It's been a couple of years since its formal adoption, and I think it's safe to say that "Circle of Friends" was always meant for Heather, Shelley, Denise, and Terry.

Of all God's gifts, certainly friendship is among the most dear. Even though I'm an only child, I have been blessed with true brothers and sisters in Christ. I'm in a weekly morning prayer group, and I have lunch once a week with a friend of fifteen years who holds me accountable, as I do him. When I read the lyric to "Circle of Friends," it immediately struck me as a song that would make people want to join hands and sing. I'm glad it has achieved that. The community and fellowship of friends is essential to my life and my relationship with God. I am thankful for the circle of friends God has given me.

Douglas McKelvey

Steve Siler

What "Circle of Friends" Means to Us

The relationship that exists within our group is special, maybe even extraordinary. I mean, after all, four girls together for eight years with no major fights? (Well, maybe one or two, but definitely fewer than I can count on one hand.) That's not just unusual; that's God.

Sharing life events has a way of cementing friendships, and we four girls have shared a lot. When I think of Denise, I think of her grace and personality. Terry is known for her caring heart, and Heather has always been synonymous with loyalty. All of these qualities join together to complete a perfect circle of friends for me.

Shelley Breen

Circles of friends are defined by varied life experiences over long periods of time. But sometimes friendships are best defined in single moments, in those shared *looks*.

The four of us have come to know each other so well, and we share such deep friendships, that we can often communicate with just a glance; a long, knowing look; or a pair of eyes rolled at just the right minute.

Sometimes when we're singing in concert and I'm going through a difficult time, it only takes a simple look from one in my circle of friends to assure me that our friendship is strong and that support is just a hug away.

Denise Jones

What "Circle of Friends" Means to Us

The first time I heard the song "Circle of Friends," I cried. I was sitting in a hotel room in Nashville, listening to the song on my little cassette player, and I thought of the girls. I knew right away that this song would mean something special for us as a group.

I'm not often overwhelmed by a song, but when I am, I know God is gently leading us toward recording it. What a joy it has been to perform this song in almost every state across America to all those huge circles of friends. I love songs that unite us girls as friends and edify the body of Christ. "Circle of Friends" has done that.

Terry Jones

Who knew that God would take four girls with big hair from Oklahoma and Arkansas and create a friendship and ministry? Only God in His wonderful sovereignty knew. I believe He predestined, even premeditated our friendship. And I am eternally thankful to Him because Terry, Shelley, and Denise are some of the best blessings in my life. Through good and bad, thick and thin (literally), our friendship has grown, not because of our own completeness, but because we are complete and whole in Christ. This book is a celebration of our friendship, our differences, and our eternal relationship.

Heather Floyd

*We were made to love
and be loved...*

$\mathcal{T}$o love and be loved

is to feel the sun

from both sides.

Barbara Johnson

YOU CAN SEARCH for something all of your life, but if you don't look in the right place, it will forever go undiscovered. For years, everything I did was driven by my search for love.

Besides looking in the wrong places, I was also looking for the wrong kind of love. The kind of "love" I sought wasn't love at all. True love gives without expecting anything in return; false love always has strings attached. And from those strings grew the bondage that plagued my life.

Instead of filling me with life, the love I sought was killing me. My heart was broken by abuse and neglect, and my soul was torn by rape. I felt alone and misunderstood. As my self-hatred grew, my wounds grew too. I cut myself, starved myself, and even tried to kill myself.

After surviving my final suicide attempt, I felt as if I had nothing left to give the world and nothing left to hope for. But in my broken state, with my shield down, God was able to come in and rescue me. What I had been searching for was there all along, but I had to choose to receive it.

God led me to a place of restoration and healing. He used Mercy Ministries of America to instill in me His unconditional, everlasting love. When I finally made the choice to full-heartedly receive His love, He gave me such an abundant supply that I now can share it with others. God has given me a new life, with new friends who share with me the greatest love of all: the love of Jesus. And together, we share the joy of lifting each other up as we serve Him and live for Him.

But the price
this world demands
will cost you
far too much...

I spent so many lonely

years just trying to fit in...

THERE'S NOTHING LIKE opening night at the Women of Faith Conferences. We speakers feel the excitement and are drawn into the thrill of God's Spirit, who is obviously at work.

After the singing, the speakers are called upon to give some opening instructions to the audience. Because our 1998 theme was Circle of Friends, our six stools were set up in a small circle on center stage. On this particular night, we each shared a few words of introduction, then passed the microphone to one of our friends.

After my turn, I backed up to hoist my five-foot frame atop my stool. I'm not sure what happened to my hoister, but it certainly fell short of the goal. Suddenly, the sitting part of my anatomy was falling to the floor at an amazing speed—taking the rest of me with it. Just inches before I splattered on the floor, hands from around the circle reached out and caught me. Those same hands then steadied me and helped me back onto the stool they had now righted. Perched where I belonged, I tried to pretend no one had noticed. (There were only fifteen thousand women in the audience.)

Jesus is our forever friend, and He helps us each time we fall. Now, He has called us to help our sisters when they fall—and trust me, sooner or later we all do. He asks us not to judge, condemn, or dishearten others but to mercifully assist our friends until they are steady and then to help them safely back into the circle.

Now I've found a place in this circle of friends...

In a circle of friends

we have one Father…

Friend

ABOUT A YEAR AGO, God placed a desire on my heart to pray for a godly, wise woman to be my prayer and account- ability partner. A woman named Brenda kept coming to mind. I hadn't talked to or seen her in quite a while, so I dismissed her from my mind.

One day as I was jogging—listening to my headphones, pretty much in my own little world—I looked up and saw a woman standing about fifty feet in front of me. It looked as if she were waiting for me. As I got closer, I realized it was Brenda. She had seen me jogging and turned her car around to talk to me. She told me she had some books she wanted me to read, and I asked her to pray about some things, then added that maybe we could get together and pray sometime. Well, sometime turned out to be soon, and we've been meeting once a week ever since.

No words can describe how our prayer time has enhanced my rela- tionship with God. Just the other day, Brenda shared a quote from Billy Graham: "Heaven is full of answers to prayers that have never been spo- ken." She said, "Heather, I want to pray those prayers." I am so thankful to Sovereign God for bringing this special friend into my life.

⚬ H e a t h e r F l o y d

WHEN HEATHER AND I gather for prayer, she often sits cross-legged on the ploppy (her word) couch, puppy Darla resting snugly against her, and I sit across from them in the large overstuffed chair by the window with the very cool plantation blinds.

We talk about what we've done and what we have failed to do. We talk about who we wish we were and who we are right now. We share requests, we confess, we cry, we believe, we pray, we travail, and we give thanks. We want to know the deep things of God.

Millions of people have heard Heather Floyd sharing and singing as a member of Point of Grace. Thousands have read magazine articles and interviews featuring Point of Grace. Yet when Heather and I gather for praise and prayer, those things go away, and we are ushered into the throne room of Holy God, who jealously waits for time with His daughters.

One time recently while Heather was praying, I opened my eyes and glanced over at her. In a few brief moments, I caught a glimpse of her fervency, her passion, her abandonment and expectation. Her voice full of emotion, with unashamed tears falling quietly, she sincerely poured out her heart to the Father. I believe I was glimpsing what Jesus sees as He leans close to hear this child's requests.

     ⑥ B r e n d a   B o s w e l l

In a circle of friends

we share this prayer...

Friend

MY GRANDMA IS THE BEST.
When I was just eight years old, I was in an
accident that almost took my life. My sisters and
I had gone to the fair and were having such a good
time until we got to the Ferris wheel. While I was standing
in line to ride it, part of a metal seat fell out of the sky and
hit me on the head. The next several minutes were a whirlwind
as I was rushed to the hospital.

When I opened my eyes, there was Grandma. She had driven
over an hour to be with me as soon as she heard about the accident.
There's just something about my grandma that fills me with peace and
comfort. I was so glad she'd come. They tell me that if the cut had been
any deeper, it would have cut my brain and perhaps taken my life.

I especially cherish the kind of friendships that share a common faith
in Christ. The heritage of faith my grandma has passed on to me is price-
less. Since birth, Grandma has been in my life—interested in everything
I'm doing, coming to all my childhood shows—showing me the love of
Christ in every instance. I am so grateful for the special friendship Grandma
and I have shared through the years. Even now, I love to just hang out with
her and soak up who she is as a grandma and a beautiful lady.

❧ T e r r y   J o n e s

WHEN TERRY WAS EIGHT years old, she and her family went to a transient carnival in their hometown. Terry and her sister, Katie, were waiting their turn to ride the Ferris wheel when, without warning, part of the metal frame fell off one of the seats high in the air and hit Terry on the head. Bleeding and in shock, Terry was rushed to a local hospital and had to get stitches in her forehead just above the right eye. The flying missile had miraculously just missed her eye. When I arrived at the hospital, I well remember the overwhelming love and relief that welled up in me when I saw that precious little girl, her right eye and forehead in a big bandage, and just the trace of a tear below her left eye.

I remember telling her then how special she was to me, but even more special to God who had protected her through this entire experience.

Whenever I see that scar on Terry's forehead, although it has faded, I thank the Lord again for her two beautiful eyes, her thankful spirit, and her warm and tender heart.

She has grown up from an adored and cherished grandchild into a dear friend—one who keeps in touch with me, shares her dreams and triumphs, and gladdens the heart of her eighty-year-old grandma, especially when I pick up the phone and hear, "Hi Gram, it's Terry."

⑥ Louise Drury, "Grandma"

*That every orphaned soul
will know
and all will
enter in...*

Two are better than one . . .

If one falls down,

his friend can help him up.

Ecclesiastes 4:9–10

To the shelter
of this circle
of friends...

S HARI WAS IN TROUBLE. I could tell by the tone of her prayers. Almost every time we talked on the phone, we would end our conversations with prayer. But one day when I called, her telephone had been disconnected, and she wasn't at church the next Sunday. I soon learned that all heck had broken out in her life. Her car had broken down. One of her relatives was in jail. Children she kept were victims of abuse. She was caring for an elderly parent. Everything was in chaos.

Yet this was the same woman who contributed to my ministry when few others were even concerned. She encouraged me when the chips were down. She counseled my children about their children and took care of other people's children as if they were her own.

How could all these bad things be happening to this good person? But each time Shari and I talked, she reminded me of how good God is, how He never makes mistakes, and how He has the answer to all our questions even before we ask. I'm blessed to have Shari in my circle of friends.

Shari and I enjoy the fellowship of eight other ladies who we've been friends with since we were in kindergarten. Each of us has an abiding relationship with the Lord. Sometimes we disagree, but we always remain agreeable. Sometimes we are burdened, but we always bear each other's burdens. Sometimes we grieve, but within our circle of friends, we always find a listening ear and an encouraging word.

*If you weep
I will weep with you...*

I T HAS BEEN SAID that there is inexpressible comfort in being able to feel safe with a friend—not having to weigh thoughts or measure words, but being allowed to pour them all right out, just as they are, chaff and grain together, knowing that she will keep what is worth keeping and, with a breath of kindness, blow the rest away.

What a blessing to have friends with whom to share our joys and our sorrows. When sorrow is shared, it is divided, and when joy is shared it is multiplied. One truth I have enjoyed sharing is that *openness is to wholeness* what *secrets are to sickness*. The full meaning of this is that we can become well by sharing our pain with a friend who can keep confidences and be understanding. A sense of wholeness and well-being results when we are able to unburden ourselves with a trusted friend.

This is how our fellowship with Christ can be. He knows our every need; He knows our limitations and our faults. What a comfort to know that when we confess our sins and receive his forgiveness, God no longer sees our sins because they are removed as far as the east is from the west.

A friend is someone who understands your past, believes in your future and accepts you just the way you are. I've heard sympathy defined as "your pain in my heart." How true that sharing our pain with our friends binds us so close to them that we experience their sorrow as our own. What a luxury it is to have friends who take our pain into their hearts. Through Christ, we have such a circle of friends.

*If you sing
for joy the rest of us
will lift our voices too...*

Sing for joy, O heavens. . .

shout aloud, O earth beneath.

Burst into song, you mountains,

you forests and all your trees.

Isaiah 44:23

Friend

I FIRST MET MARTI in the ninth grade just after my family moved from California to Oklahoma. I was so shy, but Marti took me under her wing. She was the one who convinced me to try out for the high school show choirs. Had she not pushed me, I might not be singing today.

Even though we live in different states now, we are still close. We can go weeks without talking, but when we get on the phone, we start back right where we left off.

When Chris and I broke up before we were married, Marti knew we'd get back together. When Chris and I married, Marti was our maid of honor. Then last year, just a day after Chris and I found out we were pregnant, Marti called and exclaimed that she and her husband were going to have a baby. Her due date was April 17th. Ours was April 15th!! We must have talked on the phone ten times a week to find out how the other one was feeling, to describe what we were experiencing, and to discuss what the doctor had said. We even talked in the hospital rooms as we went through labor.

Now that Marti has her sweet girl Taylor and we have our sweet boy Cole, we are sure they will one day get married.

❧ Terry Jones

IT'S BEEN FOURTEEN YEARS since Terry and I first met at Central Mid-High. I remember going home that day and telling my mom that I had met the sweetest girl. Terry always wore a big smile and never had an unkind word for anyone. We have shared so much through the years but would never have guessed that we'd share one of the happiest moments in our lives.

One evening in August, 1997, I called Terry and said, "I've got some news…" but before I could finish my sentence, Terry said, "You're pregnant!" She went on to say, "You're not going to believe this, but I just found out yesterday that I'm pregnant." Of all the things we have shared together, this was definitely the best. I bet you can guess that every phone conversation for the next nine months was baby, baby, baby. Sharing everything withTerry was so awesome because each time I called about something new—like hearing the baby's heartbeat or feeling the baby move for the first time—she knew exactly how I felt. We marveled over and over at the development of our babies. Only God could create something so amazing.

In April of 1998, God blessed us with two beautiful children. She had a boy and I a girl. Four days after she delivered her baby boy in Arkansas, I delivered my little girl in Nashville. As you might guess, both of our children are already spoken for.

⚭ M a r t i   B u s h o r e

But no matter what you feel inside there's no

need to pretend...

That's the way it is in
this circle of friends...

I BECAME A LOYAL FAN of Point of Grace the first time I saw them in concert, but when I searched the Internet for some on-line interaction with fellow fans, I discovered there was no such place. Setting up a chat room was simple, and before long, several of us who had met on-line had become fast friends and were meeting each other at concerts and visiting each other's homes. When I first meet my Internet friends face to face, we often feel as if we've known each other for years, and we talk and fellowship for hours.

Our favorite place to meet is at Point of Grace concerts. Some of us fly in, some take buses, and others drive hundreds of miles just to get there. It's always worth whatever effort we have to make to be together.

We've exchanged countless letters and packages through the mail, and we've called each other long-distance just to show we care. When one of us is feeling down, all we have to do is put our fingers to the keyboard and type, "Please pray for me. I'm going through a tough time."

Sometimes I sit and ponder how amazing it is that my little chat room has brought so many people together in such a powerful way. With so much negative talk about Internet abuse, we forget that God can also use this new medium to bring His people together. Though we were initially brought together by a common love for the music of Point of Grace, our bond as followers of Jesus Christ now holds us together in the strongest bond of all. (Come chat: www.praiseworks.com/POG)

In a circle of friends
we have one
Father.

In a
circle of friends
we share this prayer...

AFTER SEATING ME in her living room, Miss Helen picked up a small pad of yellow paper. "Now," my older friend began, "tell me everything that is bothering you, and don't stop until you're finished."

I began, and Miss Helen wrote without commentary. After about an hour, I stopped. "Is that all?" she asked.

Embarrassed, I replied, "Isn't that enough? You've almost filled that notebook!"

Then Miss Helen asked, "Do you believe God hears your prayers?"

"No," I whispered, full of shame.

"Do you believe He hears my prayers?"

"Sure!" I responded, because I had seen the amazing results of her prayers.

Her next words shocked me: "RoseAnne, I don't want you to pray; you don't believe He hears you. I will pray for you."

That hundred-pound spiritual heavyweight tore out those yellow pieces of paper and placed them in the middle of her well-worn Bible. She knelt and prayed: "Dear Lord, I know that You hear my prayers, and I come on behalf of my friend, RoseAnne. I give You all that is written on these yellow pieces of paper. They are in Your care now. Thank you for hearing the prayers of this Your servant. In Jesus' name. Amen."

I watched, Miss Helen prayed, and Jesus answered. That's what friends are for.

Friend

MY FIRST MEMORY of Sarah is in grade school. She was a tall, thin, black-headed girl with the biggest brown eyes I'd ever seen. We hit it off immediately, I guess because we were both part tomboy and enjoyed beating the boys in kickball.

We shared all sorts of secrets in the notes we passed back and forth during school, and we always ended with at least one of our favorite "codes"—LYLAS (Love Ya Like a Sister), BFF (Best Friends Forever), and SSS (Sorry So Sloppy).

One thing I can definitely say about Sarah is that she is a faithful friend. In junior high school, when I felt like a total misfit, Sarah was the one who encouraged me and made me feel included. In high school, when we experienced some big disappointments, Sarah was always there to help me laugh and cry and get through. And when my career took off with Point of Grace and I neglected our friendship for a time, she didn't hold it against me. In fact, she is one of my biggest cheerleaders. Sarah is a steadfast friend.

I plan on being friends with Sarah for the rest of my life—even for eternity. I don't deserve a friend like Sarah, but I thank my precious Lord that He has blessed me with her faithful friendship.

                               ✿ D e n i s e   J o n e s

IF YOU ARE LUCKY, you know right from the start that a new acquaintance is someone special—someone who is gentle, kind, and thoughtful; someone you can talk to and depend on. I found that special friend in Denise Jones.

I'm not sure of the exact moment when our friendship began. It may have been on one of our many walks home from school, on the softball field or basketball court, or in band class. But there is one thing I am sure of: Denise has always been there for me. With her chin held high, she taught me to never look back on what I thought were failures, but to persevere and rely on my faith.

Together, we survived elementary school, and together, we got our letter jackets in high school. We were together through our senior prom, high school graduation, and even in college. Through it all, our bond continued to grow. Now we are married and have children born nineteen days apart. As we grew up and found our places in the world, we found that we still had a place in each other.

Denise is sincere and loyal, and I'm proud to say, my best friend. I will never forget the mark she has left on my life and will always rely on what I have learned from her. Denise has given me laughter and sunshine that will be with me for the rest of my days.

⑥ S a r a h   W a t t s

*That we'll gather
together no matter how the*

highway bends...

Friend

IT WAS MY FIRST SEMESTER at college, and I hardly knew anyone. I was fast asleep in my little twin bed in my dorm room when I felt something crawling on my leg. Surely I was dreaming. Then, I felt it on my arm, but I couldn't see anything in the bed, so I tried to go back to sleep. And then it happened. Crawling across my face, *yes my face*, was a huge roach!! I sat up, screamed, and flicked it onto the floor. This gave me a case of the heebie-jeebies of the worst kind. And this roach was no small creature; it was more like a bug on major steroids. Anyhow, I was certain of this one thing: I was *not* spending the rest of the night in my bed.

The only option who came to mind was Cathy Daniel. When she answered her door, her face reflected her bewilderment. I must have looked pathetic, standing there in my jammies and clutching my blanket. "May I sleep in your bed with you tonight?" I explained that a large roach was currently borrowing mine. She kindly consented, but I know she must have been thinking, "Now, *what's* your name?" As I drifted off to sleep in her crowded bed, I thought that surely Cathy and I would become friends for life. And so we have.

                                            ☻ Shelley Breen

SHELLEY BREEN AND I MET each other when we were freshmen music majors at Ouachita Baptist University in Arkadelphia, Arkansas. We ran around with some of the same girls, but we weren't close, and we'd only visited each other's rooms a couple of times.

Then late one night, while I was sound asleep, I was awakened by a loud, obnoxious knock at my door. I couldn't imagine what was happening! When I opened the door, I found Shelley standing there with her comforter. She very dramatically explained to me that a roach had crawled across her face while she was sleeping and that she would *not* be sleeping in her room that night. I guess I was still groggy, because I somehow agreed that she could share my twin bed. Needless to say, my roommate was a bit confused when she woke up the next morning to find that Shelley had joined me during the night.

This is just one of the precious memories I have of Shelley over the past twelve years. Shelley's sense of humor and common-sense approach to problems have been a source of encouragement and much-needed laughs. I'm thankful that she is using her talents to share Jesus Christ through Point of Grace, and I'm grateful to be a part of her circle of friends.

❧ C a t h y   D a n i e l   L a y

I will not lose this circle of friends...

G UESS HOW MANY STAMPS are in my purse? Ninety-four. Before long, I'll use them to communicate with people I love.

Like Sophia. I met her thirty years ago in Athens, Greece. Since then, we've shared vacations, joys, sorrows, ups, and downs. Eight thousand miles are easily bridged with a postage stamp.

Or Kurt. During thirty-five years of traveling the world in opposite directions, we've kept in touch through letters and postcards. At the bottom, those three little words "I love you" and his illegible signature feed my soul.

And Charlotte. I rarely see her, but the postcards I write from everywhere keep our forty-year friendship current.

Staying in touch is in my genes. My garage houses mountains of mail from my family. (Recently I found a yellowed note in my grandmother's pile: "Gone next door to borrow an egg." And I can't throw it away!)

Now I've gone electronic. Between Florida and California, Debbie and I meet in cyberspace daily. Friends with whom I share the strongest bond and deepest affection are not necessarily those in the closest proximity but those who value communication, even if it's long-distance. It takes time but has immeasurable rewards.

Someday I won't be traveling with Point of Grace. When that sad day comes I have three little words for them: "Stay in touch." Time and distance need not separate friends. Got stamps?

Among the nations, tribes and tongues we have sisters and brothers...

I MET HER for the first time when she was six years old. I told the people at Compassion International, a ministry of Christian child development, that I wanted to sponsor a little girl who lived in a country I could visit. Six months later, I made my first trip to Ecuador to meet Gavi.

I flipped out when I saw her. She had big, brown eyes; a beautiful, smooth complexion; and a smile that lit up her face. Although she was shy and unsure of herself, she immediately took my hand and didn't let go the whole day. A friendship was born that has grown ever since.

I've learned a lot from Gavi over the years. But the lesson that's impacted me the most was painful to learn. In Gavi's culture, when a girl turns fifteen, a big celebration—a *quinceñera*—is held in honor of her becoming a woman. Months before the big event, Gavi asked me to come, and I told her I'd try. And I did try. But my schedule was especially crazy when it came time to go, and I had to cancel.

The next time I visited Gavi, we were interviewed together, and as usual, Gavi was holding my hand. As she was talking to the interviewer, a cloud came over Gavi's otherwise bright face, and big tears began to roll down her cheeks. Through an interpreter I learned that Gavi was explaining how sad she'd felt when I missed her *quinceñera*. I knew at that moment that I'd made the wrong choice. Whatever had been going on in my world was not as important as Gavi.

Gavi is now eighteen years old. She graduated from high school last month—and I was there. I even got to present her diploma.

Communion

I WAS BONE TIRED by the time I stepped off the plane in Estonia and more than a little grateful to have arrived safely. My flight on the Russian airline, Aeroflot (I renamed it Aeroflop), was something you would have to experience to believe. I had no seat belt, a large, ugly dog drooled on my suede boots, and a drunken soldier deposited himself on my right shoulder. As I staggered into the terminal, I saw their faces. A large group of women from the local churches was there to meet me. Many of them pulled me into their arms and kissed both my cheeks.

I spoke no Estonian, and they spoke no English, except for one little old lady who grasped my hand and whispered in my ear, "God is good." I smiled a halfhearted smile, worried about the language barrier and how we would communicate. But as I looked across the faces of these dear women, I realized that in the Spirit there was no language barrier. I was there to work side by side with them to share the radical love and grace of God in the first ever Christian concert in Estonia, which was being held in the Communist party headquarters!

"Now we thank!" the old lady at my side whispered in my ear. As one, they knelt right there in the baggage claim area and raised their hearts and voices to our Lord.

"God is good, yes?" She looked into my eyes, and her smile lit up her face like the Fourth of July.

"Yes," I replied with tears rolling down my face, "God is good."

*And when we meet
in heaven, we will
recognize each other...*

WHEN PATRICIO STOPPED BY our Nashville office with a stack of beautifully done translations of some of my songs, my brother and manager, David, knew that God had sent an answer to prayer.

I had grown up as a missionary's child in Argentina, and after struggling through a period of rebellion, I sensed a calling to minister to Spanish people through my music. We had gone to the Lord for guidance, and He sent us Patricio, an Argentine missionary to Mexico.

Our relationship with Patricio grew over time, and our ministry was privileged to support him financially. When he invited us to tour three cities in Mexico, we eagerly agreed. His desire to impact the communities was sincere, and he expected the largest arena in Mexico City to sell out.

But somewhere along the way, we became apprehensive. The ticket prices seemed exorbitant, even higher than U.S. concerts, and we couldn't get concrete answers about ticket sales and tour expenses. Patricio's reply over the phone was repeatedly, *"No se preocupe"*—"Don't worry."

When we arrived in Mexico, the situation was as we had feared. What Patricio meant as assurance, "Everything is fine; don't worry," we interpreted as indisclosure. By the conclusion of the trip, we were disappointed, and he was embarrassed. A few weeks later, we withdrew our support, expressing concern about his lack of accountability and submission to a board of authority. We were sure it was the right thing to do.

A couple of years later, we received a letter from Patricio. His words pierced like a knife, each carefully crafted sentence finding its mark and making its point. These were serious accusations about grave offenses; they could not be taken lightly.

Through prayer, the Lord directed me to Matthew 5:23–24: "If you are offering your gift at the altar and there remember that your brother has something against you, leave your gift, . . . go and be reconciled to your brother." How could I continue with concerts and worship when a brother was deeply offended?

I knew that nothing less than a face-to-face meeting would do. We called and asked Patricio if he would allow us to fly him to Nashville. He agreed. By the time the day arrived, God had done His work in me, convicting me of judgment instead of mercy, of condemnation instead of love.

Defenses down and behind closed doors, we confessed our sins, and the walls of hurt were torn down as Christ's love drew us together. With tears, embraces, and words of affection, our friendship was mended and restored.

Today, Patricio is one of my most treasured friends. We have vowed to never again let misunderstandings and wrongs build a wall between us but, instead, to keep the unity of the Spirit in the bond of peace. We reinstated our support of Patricio and are thrilled to be a part of what God is doing in that part of the world.

With joy so deep and love so sweet, Oh, we'll celebrate these friends and a life that never ends...

*P*rayers have no boundaries.

They can leap miles and

continents and be translated

instantly into any language.

Billy Graham

In a circle of friends

we have one Father...

"I CAN'T STAND UP, Daddy, my legs quit working!" I narrowly avoided stumbling over the little roadblock who suddenly plopped down in front of me in the mall. Her daddy smiled at me apologetically and then stooped down to inquire about his little girl's sudden paralysis.

"My legs are too tired to walk anymore. I think they need some ice cream." I was sufficiently intrigued to slow my pace. Her loving daddy scooped her up into his arms, and as they walked away, I heard her say, "Daddy, I'm pretty sure your legs need some ice cream too."

A couple of days ago I had an undramatic little surgery that required a general anesthetic. When I tried to get to the car chauffeured by my friend Pat, my legs wouldn't work. Climbing awkwardly into the front seat of her car, I remembered the little darling at the mall who had the perfect solution for legs that didn't work. Employing the same strategy as my little friend, I said, "You know, Pat, I'm not sure I'll be able to walk into the house in my present condition."

"Really, honey," she said sympathetically, "I'm sure I can help you."

"Well, I've heard that the best cure for legs that don't work is ice cream."

Later, as we watched reruns of *The Golden Girls* and slurped ice cream together, Pat said, "You know, my legs feel better too!"

Don't you love friends who enter into your experience to share both your pain and your joy? That's what I call a double-dip!

*In a
circle of friends
we share this prayer...*

Friend

ONE OF THE GREATEST JOYS experienced by humans is witnessing a friend or loved one become a Christian. Greater still is being a tool in God's hand used to share His love and plan of eternal salvation with that person. God's miracle of transformation is truly a joy to behold.

I met Nicole at a summer camp when we were both kids. Fifteen years later, our paths crossed again through a Christian gal friend of mine named Sami. The three of us began hanging out together. We went to dinner, movies, and pool parties. Nicole had attended a Christian college on a gymnastics scholarship and, after four years of required Bible classes and chapel services, perceived Christianity and Christians to be boring and weird. But now, her perception of Christians was beginning to change.

Nicole would often just listen as Sami and I talked about the Lord and what Jesus meant to us. Christianity was often talked about but never preached. Nicole was searching but had never been confronted with choosing to accept or reject the person Jesus Christ. But at a Labor Day conference in 1995, Nicole found out what she was searching for—Jesus Christ. Since then, Nicole has taken the gospel message to her workplace, the gym, and even the streets of Houston, proclaiming that Christianity is not boring or weird but a miracle from God.

❧ M a r c   K o h l e r

As far back as I can remember, I have always felt in control of my life. But at age twenty-six, I realized I was unhappy and lonely; and I was beginning to burn out on the nightclub scene. I ran into a girl I used to know from the party scene named Sami. She told me she had recently become involved in church. Soon, Sami introduced me to Marc, and we discovered that he and I had gone to summer camp together when I was ten years old.

Over the next few months, Sami, Marc, and I began spending time together. Sometimes I would meet them for dinner and then later connect with my other friends at a nightclub. Though my lifestyle was different from theirs, Sami and Marc were never judgmental. Sometimes Marc would share what God was doing in his life and how awesome it was to have a relationship with Jesus Christ. I thought he was a little weird, yet I enjoyed spending time with him.

That same summer, Marc and Sami invited me to go to Destin, Florida, for a Christian Conference for singles (not my idea of a vacation). The evening Point of Grace performed, I gave my life to Jesus Christ.

I am now married to a godly man and am involved in my church. If someone had told me four years ago that Jesus Christ would be the number one priority in my life, I never would have believed it. God really does have a sense of humor!

⑥ N i c o l e   S e l f

That it will not be long before all will enter in to the shelter of this circle of friends.

I AM CONVINCED there are times when God purposely distances us from our friends. He never intends that we feel forsaken. His purpose is to introduce *Himself* as a *friend who is closer than a brother.*

Several years ago, God ushered me into a season of aloneness. During this time, I cried out to Him, "Lord, I am nearly dying of loneliness!" Over and over, He spoke to my heart, "Child, I will give you back old friends and new, but right now, *I* want to be your Friend."

One cold night when no one else was home, I grabbed my headphones, put in a worship tape, and went for a walk through a park across from our home. Tears poured down my face, but I kept repeating to God, "I love You; I trust You. You know what is best for me." Step by step, the praises feeding my spirit became my own. The love and presence of God consumed me. My heart was so overcome with worship that I stopped right in the middle of the park, lifted my hands, and sang praises to Him. As I stared upward, God sent a flash of lightning across the sky. I sang another phrase, and as if in response, He sent the lightning again. Then God's voice took on the sound of distant thunder, and I believe with all my heart that He was singing over me. As we "sang" back and forth to one another, I was amazed at what the God of the universe was willing to do for one child. That memory will last a lifetime.

God graciously gives us the joy of friendship, but every now and then, His mighty hand pushes our loved ones back to make room for *Himself.*

Also available from Point of Grace

The song "Circle of Friends" is also available on the CD
Life, Love, and Other Mysteries

CD, 7464 67698 2

Steady On
The Book
Hardcover, ISBN 1-878990-93-4

Steady On
The Music
8068 85444 2

Book and CDs available at your local Christian bookstore.